MENTAL HEALTH IS A LIE

Why You Haven't Healed Yet—And the Missing Piece No One Taught You

BY MAXIMUS LEROIS
PSYCHOTHERAPIST

DISCLAIMER

The advice contained in this material might not be suitable for everyone. The authors designed the information to present their opinion about the subject matter. The reader must carefully investigate all aspects of any business decision before committing to him or herself. The authors obtained the information contained herein from sources they believe to be reliable and from their own personal experiences, but they neither imply nor intend any guarantee of accuracy. The authors are not in the business of giving legal, accounting, or any other type of professional advice. Should the reader need such advice, they must seek services from a competent professional. The authors particularly disclaim any liability, loss, or risk taken by individuals who directly or indirectly act on the information contained herein. The authors believe the advice presented here is sound and reliable. Still, readers cannot hold them responsible for either the actions they take or the risks taken by individuals who directly or indirectly act on the information contained herein.

Published by 1Brick Publishing

Printed in the United States

Copyright © 2025 by Maximus Lerois

ISBN 978-1949303421

DEDICATION

To my 16-year-old self — we did it.

Table of Contents

The Truth That Will Set You Free

I'll never forget standing before a room full of college students at a mental health awareness event in Chicago.

I looked out at their faces—some tired, some anxious, some pretending to be fine—and I dropped the line that made the whole room freeze:

"Mental health is a lie."

You could feel the silence stretch across the room. A few counselors in the back shifted in their seats. Some students frowned. Others looked uncertain—like they wanted to agree but didn't know if they were allowed to. Then something shifted. Eyes lifted. Shoulders leaned forward. Curiosity cracked through the discomfort.

That's because deep down, most of us already know it: we've been told to "manage" our mental health for years... yet we're still hurting. Still anxious. Still searching for peace that actually lasts.

Mental Health Isn't Wrong—It's Incomplete

Let me be clear: I'm not here to bash mental health. I'm a psychotherapist, a certified practitioner in both emotional intelligence (EQ) and Neuro-Linguistic Programming (NLP), and a Marine veteran who's spent years studying resilience. I know therapy and medication save lives.

But if you've ever wondered why you're *still* stuck—still anxious, still carrying depression, still battling old trauma—it's because the picture you've been given is only half the truth.

Mental health focuses on the mind. But most of what keeps us stuck isn't in our thoughts—it's in our nervous system, our bodies, and our inherited patterns.

That's where **emotional intelligence** comes in. EQ doesn't replace mental health—it completes it. Together, they provide us with the complete map to healing.

You Don't Just Think Anxiety—You Feel It Too

Think about the last time you felt anxious. Did it start only in your thoughts? Or in your chest? Your stomach? Your breath?

You don't just *think* about anxiety. You *feel* it too.

That's because emotions don't live in your head—they live in your body. Anxiety is a tightness in the chest. Depression is heaviness in the bones. Trauma is a nervous system stuck in a state of survival mode.

Until we address emotional pain where it lives—in the body and nervous system—we're just managing symptoms instead of healing the root.

You are not broken. You are becoming.

MY BACKPACK OF BURDENS

I learned this the hard way.

Growing up in South Los Angeles, I was the kid who loved anime and comic books in a neighborhood where survival meant being hard. My family on both sides was deep in gang culture, and there was no way little old me was going to change it. So, I decided to take a different path—I joined the Marines.

Two deployments later, I was decorated, disciplined, and broken inside. Not because I was weak, but because I was carrying more than my share.

Anxiety before every mission. Rage when my authority was questioned. Sleepless nights long after I got home. None of it started with me—it was my grandmother's fear, my father's anger, my ancestors' survival instincts... all packed into a backpack I never asked to carry.

The turning point came when I realized this simple truth: **I could put the backpack down.**

A NEW WAY FORWARD

What I've built since then isn't about bashing therapy, medication, or mental health awareness. It's about showing the missing part of the picture—the piece that makes all the difference.

Over the past decade, I've developed something I call **SoulScience Alchemy™**—a practical framework that combines neuroscience, psychotherapy, and emotional intelligence. It's designed to do more than manage pain. It helps you:

- **Recognize** the hidden "soul weights" keeping you stuck.
- **Reframe** pain into purpose.
- **Release** what was never yours to carry.

This isn't about quick fixes or endless coping. It's about real healing—healing that lasts.

Who This Book is For

This book is for anyone who's ever felt broken by their diagnosis, anyone who's been managing but not healing, anyone tired of carrying pain in silence.

It's for the therapist who knows their clients deserve more.
It's for the soldier who came home but still feels at war.
It's for the achiever who looks "successful" but feels empty inside.
It's for you—because you are not broken. You are becoming.

The Truth That Will Set You Free

Some of what you read in these pages may challenge you. It might even make you uncomfortable. That's good. Discomfort means that something inside you is awakening.

Here's my promise: If you stick with me, if you're willing to go beyond managing symptoms and start listening to your body, you'll discover that healing isn't just possible—it's your birthright.

This is your invitation to step back, see the whole picture, and finally put the pack down.

Mental health is a lie. Emotional wellness is the truth. It's time to heal.

Maximus Lerois
"We Heal Out Loud Every Day"

PART I:
SEEING THE WHOLE PICTURE

WHAT YOU DON'T RELEASE, YOU REPEAT.

#AWHOLEMOMENT

CHAPTER 1

Mental Health Is a Lie — Here's the Missing Piece

"You do not have a mental illness. You're emotionally overwhelmed by a nervous system stuck in survival mode."

Most people consider healing a mental process. You sit in therapy, you talk it out, you try to think your way into feeling better. But here's the truth:

You don't think about anxiety.
You feel it.

You don't think of depression.
You feel it.

You don't think trauma.
You feel it.

The lie isn't that mental health doesn't matter—it does. The lie is that it's the *whole* picture.

THE 70/30 RULE

Neuroscience has revealed something startling yet simple: approximately **70% of our daily actions and responses stem from subconscious emotional patterns** ingrained in the brain and nervous system. Only **30% comes from conscious thought.**

That means most of what drives your behavior isn't logic, reason, or "mental health"—it's emotion, sensation, and survival instinct.

So when you try to solve emotional pain by thinking harder, analyzing deeper, or managing symptoms at the mental level... you're working with the 30% and ignoring the 70%.

That's like trying to fix a flood by mopping the floor while leaving the broken pipe untouched.

THE BODY KEEPS THE FEELINGS FIRST

Anxiety isn't a thought problem—it's your nervous system sensing threat.
Depression isn't always a chemical imbalance—it can be your body going into shutdown mode to conserve energy. Trauma isn't "all in your head"—it's a survival imprint written into your body.

This isn't self-help talk. This is hard science. Researchers like Dr. Stephen Porges (Polyvagal Theory) have proven that the body responds first, the brain second. Your survival brain and emotional brain fire long before your rational brain comes online.

That's why you can *feel* safe but still experience panic.
That's why you can *understand* your trauma and still feel triggered.
That's why you can *think positively* but still feel heavy.

Because feelings don't live in your head, they live in your nervous system.

THE MISSING PIECE: EMOTIONAL INTELLIGENCE

This is where emotional intelligence (EQ) comes in.

EQ isn't about crying on cue or being "touchy-feely." It's the ability to:

- Recognize what you're actually feeling.
- Regulate your nervous system when it's overwhelmed.
- Reframe experiences so your emotions serve you, not sabotage you.
- Release what was never yours to carry in the first place.

Mental health focuses on the thoughts. EQ focuses on feelings. Together, they provide the *complete* picture.

TRY THIS RIGHT NOW

Let's make this real. Think about the last time you felt stressed or anxious. Don't overanalyze—just pick a moment.

Now, scan your body:

- Was it tightness in your chest?
- A knot in your stomach?
- Tension in your jaw?
- Shallow breathing?
- Notice where it lived.

Here's the insight: That's your nervous system talking. It's not random. It's not a weakness. It's your body's intelligent way of keeping score.

And when you learn to listen to these signals instead of ignoring them, you unlock the power to heal at the root—not just manage symptoms.

THE BIG SHIFT

For too long, we've been told to fix everything from the neck up. But healing doesn't start in the head—it begins in the body.

This doesn't mean therapy and medication are useless. They save lives. But by themselves, they're incomplete. **Mental health gives you part of the picture. emotional intelligence gives you the rest.**

And when you put those pieces together, something powerful happens:

- Anxiety becomes information, not identity.
- Depression becomes a signal, not a life sentence.
- Trauma becomes fuel for transformation, rather than dead weight in your backpack.
- That's the work we're about to do together.

THE NEUROSCIENCE BEHIND IT

- **70/30 Rule:** Approximately 70% of behavior is driven by subconscious emotional patterns, while 30% is influenced by conscious thought. (Research: Stanford, NIMH, Harvard).
- **Polyvagal Theory:** Dr. Stephen Porges showed that our nervous system has three states:
    - *Ventral Vagal (Safety):* calm, connected, social.
    - *Sympathetic (Mobilization):* fight-or-flight.
    - *Dorsal Vagal (Shutdown):* freeze, numb, depressed.

- Most "mental health symptoms" are really signs that we're stuck in *survival mode*
- Healing isn't about erasing these states—it's about learning to regulate and return to a state of safety.

SoulScience Alchemy in Action: Marcus's Breakthrough

Marcus had been in therapy for three years for anxiety and depression. He'd tried multiple medications and coping strategies. Nothing stuck.

In our first session, instead of asking about his *thoughts*, I asked about his *body*. He said, "My chest feels tight. My stomach feels like it's full of concrete."

We didn't try to make the feelings go away. We listened. We let his body tell the story. And that's when Marcus realized: his "anxiety" wasn't illness—it was his body screaming at him to stop living for other people's expectations.

The shift wasn't intellectual. It was emotional. It was nervous system deep. And for the first time in years, Marcus felt relief.

DROP THE PACK: THE NERVOUS SYSTEM CHECK-IN

Try this exercise the next time you feel stress:

1. Sit quietly. Bring to mind something mildly stressful.
2. Instead of analyzing it, scan your body.
3. Notice:
   - Where do you feel tightness?
   - Where do you feel heaviness?
   - Where do you feel constriction?
   - Place your hand gently on that area.
4. Say: *"I notice you. What are you trying to tell me?"*
5. Breathe slowly. Don't fix—just listen.
6. Thank your nervous system for trying to protect you.
7. This practice shifts you from "thinking your feelings" to *feeling your feelings.* That's where real healing begins.

CHAPTER 1 KEY TAKEAWAYS

- Subconscious emotional patterns drive 70% of your life.
- Emotions don't live in your head—they live in your nervous system.
- Mental health addresses thoughts. emotional intelligence addresses feelings. Together, they create wholeness.
- Anxiety, depression, and trauma are signals—not life sentences.
- Healing starts by noticing and listening to the body.

CHAPTER 2

You're Not Broken — You're Carrying Someone Else's Backpack

"We're running the trauma Olympics, and our parents are handing off the stick. You can stop the race and walk off the field."

S ometimes the heaviest weight you carry isn't even yours.

You look at your life and think: *"I should be fine. Why do I feel like I'm drowning?"* The answer may be simple: you're carrying burdens passed down long before you ever took a breath.

MY GRANDMOTHER'S HANDS

I was eight years old, sitting at my great-grandmother's kitchen table in Compton, watching her cook breakfast. Her hands shook every time she reached for the coffee pot. Every time a car backfired outside, I jumped out of my chair like someone had fired a gun in the room. I was curious to know why she would look so concerned whenever my cousin Glen and I went outside. She would give us a full rundown of what to do, where we could and couldn't go, and how to act if the police spoke to us. And she always looked so concerned that her hands would shake when she saw us heading to the door. One day, I finally stopped and asked her.

"Grandma, why do your hands do that?" I asked.

She paused for a moment and looked at me with tired eyes that held decades of stories she'd never tell.

"Baby," she said softly, "some things just get passed down."

I didn't understand it then. But years later—standing in my own kitchen, hands shaking after another sleepless night filled with Afghanistan flashbacks—I knew exactly what she meant.

Trauma travels. And sometimes, it shows up in our bodies before we ever know its name.

THE BACKPACK NOBODY TALKS ABOUT

Picture this: You're born into this world carrying a backpack. But it's not empty. It's already packed with rocks that your parents put there. Rocks that their parents put in their backpacks. Rocks that have been passed down through generations like some twisted family heirloom.

The rock labeled "Men don't cry" from your father, who learned it from his father, who learned it from his father during the Great Depression.

The rock labeled "The world is dangerous" was given to you by your mother, who inherited it from her mother, who lived through war, poverty, or abuse.

The rock labeled "You're not good enough" from family members who never learned they were worthy of love because nobody ever taught them they were.

You've been carrying other people's trauma since the day you were born, and nobody ever told you that you could set it down.

This isn't a metaphor. This isn't therapy speak. This is neuroscience.

Researchers at places like Mount Sinai School of Medicine have proven that trauma literally changes our DNA. They call it epigenetic inheritance — the biological mechanism through which the effects of trauma can be passed from one generation to the next.

Children of Holocaust survivors carry genetic markers of their parents' trauma. Descendants of enslaved people show measurable stress responses to situations their ancestors experienced generations ago. Kids who grow up in poverty develop nervous systems that are hypervigilant for scarcity, even when they achieve financial success as adults.

Your anxiety might not be yours. Your depression might be inherited. Your trauma responses might be genetic hand-me-downs that don't even fit your actual life.

Shame hands you the pack. Healing teaches you to set it down.

#AWHOLEMOMENT

THE FAMILY OPERATING SYSTEM

Every family has what I call an "emotional operating system" — a set of unspoken rules about how feelings are handled, what's safe to express, and what needs to be buried.

In my family, the operating system was simple: Survive by any means necessary. Don't show weakness. Don't trust outsiders. Don't expect life to be fair.

These weren't conscious decisions. They were survival strategies that got encoded into our nervous systems over generations of living in environments where being vulnerable could literally get you killed.

My great-grandfather grew up in the Jim Crow South, where showing the wrong emotion to the wrong person could end your life. That hypervigilance, that constant scanning for threats, that inability to fully relax — it got passed down to my grandfather, then to my father, then to me.

By the time it reached me, I was living in a completely different world. I had opportunities my ancestors could never have imagined. But my nervous system was still running on software designed for surviving racial terrorism in 1920s Mississippi.

I was trying to live a 2020s life with a 1920s nervous system.

THE INVISIBLE INHERITANCE

Here's what's insidious about inherited trauma: You don't even know you're carrying it. It feels like it's just "who you are."

You think you're naturally anxious. You think you're just a worrier. You think you have trust issues because of your own experiences.

But what if your anxiety is actually your grandmother's unprocessed fear from living through the Great Depression?

What if your inability to relax comes from your grandfather's war trauma that he never talked about?

What if your perfectionism is really your mother's inherited belief that love has to be earned through achievement?

Let me tell you about Maria, one of my clients. She came to me because she couldn't stop working. Successful entrepreneur, beautiful family, financial freedom — but she was working 80-hour weeks and couldn't figure out why she was so driven to keep hustling even when she had enough.

In our third session, we started exploring her family history. Her grandmother had come to America with nothing, worked multiple jobs to feed her kids, and lived in constant fear of not having enough. Her mother had inherited that same drive, that same fear of scarcity, that same belief that rest equals danger.

Maria wasn't working 80 hours a week because she needed to. She was working 80 hours a week because her nervous system had inherited the belief that slowing down meant starvation.

Once she recognized this pattern, she could start making conscious choices instead of unconscious reactions. She could honor her grandmother's survival strength while choosing to live from abundance instead of scarcity.

THE NERVOUS SYSTEM'S MEMORY BANK

Your nervous system doesn't distinguish between your trauma and your ancestors' trauma. It doesn't care if the danger happened to you personally or to someone you're biologically connected to. All it knows is: "This pattern helped someone in our family line survive. Better keep it active just in case."

That's why you can feel anxious in objectively safe situations. Your rational brain knows you're fine, but your nervous system is responding to threats that your great-grandmother faced decades ago.

That's why certain emotions feel forbidden in your body. Not because you decided they were dangerous, but because expressing them wasn't safe for someone in your family system generations back.

That's why some people feel guilty for being happy, prosperous, or peaceful. Their nervous system equates ease with danger because their ancestors never had the luxury of feeling safe.

THE GENERATIONAL RELAY RACE

I want you to imagine trauma as a relay race. Each generation runs its leg of the race carrying a baton loaded with unprocessed pain, survival strategies, and coping mechanisms.

Your great-grandparents ran their leg through war, poverty, discrimination, or abuse. They developed incredible strength and resilience, but they also carried wounds they never had the opportunity to heal.

Your grandparents took the baton and ran their leg through their own challenges — maybe economic instability, social upheaval, or family dysfunction. They added their own survival strategies to the baton while carrying forward what they inherited.

Your parents took that baton and ran their leg through the unique challenges of their generation. They did the best they could with the tools they had, but they were still carrying the accumulated weight of everyone who came before them.

Then they handed the baton to you.

But here's what nobody ever told you: You don't have to keep running the race.

You can stop. You can set the baton down. You can choose to heal what got passed down instead of passing it forward.

This isn't about blaming your parents or ancestors. They were doing the best they could with the resources at their disposal. Many of the survival strategies they developed were necessary and life-saving in their context.

But their context isn't your context. Their challenges aren't your challenges. Their limitations don't have to be your limitations.

THE FAMILY TRAUMA AUDIT

Let's do something together. I want you to reflect on the emotional patterns that emerge within your family system. Not just your immediate family, but going back as far as you can remember or have heard stories about.

What were the unspoken rules in your family about:

- Expressing anger?
- Showing vulnerability?
- Asking for help?
- Celebrating success?
- Handling conflict?
- Trusting outsiders?
- Managing money?
- Showing affection?

What survival strategies did your family develop around:

- Safety and security?
- Love and relationships?
- Work and achievement?
- Health and self-care?
- Spirituality and meaning?

What stories do you carry about:

- What does it mean to be a man/woman in your family?
- What's possible for people like you?
- How much happiness/success/peace are you allowed to have?
- What do you have to do to earn love and belonging?

As you answer these questions, notice what feels heavy in your body. Notice what makes your chest tighten or your stomach clench. Notice what brings up resistance or defensiveness.

Those are the rocks in your backpack that don't belong to you.

THE DIFFERENCE BETWEEN YOURS AND THEIRS

Here's how to tell the difference between your authentic emotions and inherited trauma patterns:

Your authentic emotions:

- Have a clear connection to present-moment circumstances
- Feel proportional to what's actually happening
- Move through your system when processed
- Lead to insight and resolution
- Feel like they belong to you

Inherited trauma patterns:

- Feel disproportionate to current circumstances
- Seem to come out of nowhere
- Feel familiar and repetitive
- Don't resolve through standard processing
- Feel like they're happening to you, but are not from you

Let me give you an example. If you get anxious before job interviews because you want to make a good impression, that's your authentic emotion responding to a current situation.

However, if you become panicked every time you have to speak up in a meeting, even when you know your material and the environment is supportive. That might be a result of inherited shame about taking up space or being seen — something that wasn't safe for someone in your family line.

THE ENERGETIC INHERITANCE

This goes deeper than just learned behaviors or genetic predispositions. Families also pass down what I call "energetic inheritance" — the emotional frequency or vibration that the family system operates from.

Some families operate from a state of scarcity — there's never enough time, money, love, or safety. Even when circumstances improve, the family system maintains that frequency of lack.

Some families operate from a state of hypervigilance — constantly scanning for threats, unable to relax, and assuming that danger is always lurking.

Some families operate from emotional suppression — feelings are dangerous, vulnerability is weakness, the safe thing is to stay numb.

These energetic patterns get transmitted through the nervous system faster than thought, more completely than words, more persistently than conscious intention.

You can inherit your family's emotional frequency the same way you inherit their eye color — automatically, unconsciously, completely.

BREAKING THE CYCLE

The beautiful thing about recognizing inherited patterns is that recognition itself begins to break their hold over you.

When you realize that your anxiety might be your grandmother's unprocessed trauma, something shifts. You can start relating to it in a different way. Instead of "I'm an anxious person," you can think, "I'm carrying my grandmother's anxiety, and I can choose to heal it."

When you understand that your workaholic tendencies may be a form of inherited survival programming, you can start making conscious choices about how you want to work, rather than being driven by unconscious compulsions.

When you see that your difficulty with intimacy might be your family's protective strategy around vulnerability, you can start experimenting with different ways of connecting.

You can hold onto the strength, wisdom, and resilience of your ancestors while releasing the trauma, limitations, and survival strategies that no longer serve you.

THE HEALING RIPPLE EFFECT

Here's something powerful: When you heal inherited trauma patterns, you don't just heal yourself. You heal backward through your family line and forward into future generations.

When you break the cycle of anxiety, your children won't inherit that pattern from you.

When you transform inherited shame into self-worth, you change the family's emotional operating system.

When you turn survival mode into thriving mode, you give your descendants a different foundation to build from.

Your healing doesn't just impact you; it also impacts those around you. It affects everyone who came before you and everyone who comes after you.

THE ANCESTOR APPRECIATION PRACTICE

Before we move on to releasing inherited patterns, I want you to do something important: honor the strength of your ancestors.

Every survival strategy they developed, every protective pattern they created, every way they learned to cope — these things kept your family line alive long enough for you to be here.

Your grandmother's hypervigilance might have protected her children from real danger.

Your grandfather's emotional shutdown might have helped him survive trauma that would have broken other people.

Your parents' workaholism might have provided the stability that gave you opportunities they never had.

These patterns served their purpose. They no longer need to serve that purpose.

You can honor the survival wisdom of your ancestors while choosing to live from a place of thriving instead of just surviving.

You can appreciate their strength while releasing their limitations.

You can carry forward their love while setting down their trauma.

THE NEUROSCIENCE BEHIND IT

Epigenetic Inheritance Research:

Studies on Holocaust survivors and their children showed that trauma can literally alter gene expression in ways that get passed to the next generation. The children of trauma survivors showed:

- Altered stress hormone levels
- Heightened fear responses
- Changes in genes linked to stress regulation

Dr. Rachel Yehuda's research at Mount Sinai proved that trauma doesn't just affect the people who experience it directly — it affects their children and grandchildren through epigenetic changes that can persist for generations.

Mirror Neuron Transmission:

Children don't just learn family patterns through instruction — they absorb them through mirror neurons that automatically mimic the nervous system states of their caregivers. A chronically anxious parent literally transmits that nervous system state to their child through neurological resonance.

SOULSCIENCE ALCHEMY IN ACTION: DAVID'S LIBERATION

David came to me with what he called "inherited workaholism." His grandfather worked three jobs during the Depression. His father built a business but never enjoyed it. By 35, David was financially free—but still grinding 70 hours a week.

Through his work, he realized he was carrying the baton of their scarcity. He honored their strength, but chose not to repeat their suffering. Within months, he cut his hours in half—without losing income.

"I can honor their sacrifice," he told me, "without reliving it."

DROP THE PACK: THE FAMILY PATTERN AUDIT

Exercise: Mapping Your Emotional Inheritance

Part 1: The Family Emotional Rules

Write down the unspoken rules in your family about:

- When/how to express anger
- How to handle conflict

- What emotions are "acceptable" for your gender
- How to respond to success or failure
- What it means to be strong/weak

Part 2: The Inherited Patterns

For each rule, ask yourself:

- Does this pattern serve my current life?
- Where do I feel this pattern in my body?
- What would change if I didn't carry this pattern?

Part 3: The Appreciation Practice

For patterns you want to release:

- How did this pattern serve your ancestors?
- What strength or wisdom does it represent?
- How can you honor that wisdom while choosing differently?

Part 4: The Conscious Choice Complete this statement for each pattern: *"I appreciate how [pattern] helped my family survive [circumstance]. I choose to honor that strength by [new choice] instead of repeating [old pattern]."*

The insight: Most of your emotional patterns aren't yours. They're survival strategies inherited from people who lived in entirely different circumstances. You can honor their wisdom while selecting responses that align with your actual life.

Chapter 2 Key Takeaways:

- Trauma travels through generations via epigenetic inheritance and nervous system transmission
- Many of your emotional patterns are inherited survival strategies, not personal pathology
- You can honor ancestral strength while releasing outdated protective mechanisms
- Healing inherited patterns affects past and future generations, not just you
- Recognition of inherited patterns is the first step toward conscious choice

CHAPTER 3

Why the current model keeps you stuck

I f you've ever sat in therapy year after year, filled prescriptions, learned coping skills, and still woken up heavy—you are not the problem.

The truth is straightforward: Mental health care, as it's traditionally built, was designed more to manage symptoms than to facilitate full healing. Management has value. It can keep you safe in a storm. But a life jacket isn't the same as a boat. This chapter is about building the ship.

MANAGEMENT VS. HEALING

How the model usually goes:

- You feel anxious, depressed, and overwhelmed.
- You're evaluated, given a diagnosis, and a care plan is created.
- You learn coping skills, maybe start medication, and attend sessions.
- You function better... but the root remains.

- That is **management**—stabilizing symptoms enough to get through the day. Necessary? Sometimes, absolutely. Sufficient? Not if you want freedom.

Healing means changing the patterns at the level where they live—your body, emotions, and nervous system—so the same triggers no longer run the same loops. Healing isn't "perfect." Its **capacity**: more room to feel, choose, connect, and rise.

Keep what helps you function. Add what sets you free.

Good People, Incomplete System

Most clinicians care deeply. Many lives have been saved—including mine and those of people I love. The challenge isn't the hearts in the room; it's the **shape of the room**: short appointments, insurance rules, symptom checklists, and a brain-first bias that often leaves the **nervous system** out of the conversation.

This chapter isn't about blame. It's about **completing the picture** so you can finally move.

The Pathology Trap (When Labels Become Cages)

Labels can offer language, validation, and access to care. They can also quietly shift your identity from *"I feel anxious"* to *"I am an anxious person."* From *"I'm in a season of depression"* to *"I have depression."*

Two truths can coexist:

- A diagnosis can describe real patterns.
- A diagnosis is not your destiny.
- Use labels like **maps**, not **mirrors**. Helpful for orientation—dangerous as identity.

A gentle reframing:

> *"I'm noticing patterns of anxiety in my body and life right now. I'm learning to work with them."*

THE MEDICATION LOOP (BREATHING ROOM VS. BREAKTHROUGH)

Medication can be a lifeline. It can calm a storm, create stability, and save lives. Honor that. Also, note this: medications typically **modulate symptoms**; they rarely **resolve the root cause**.

- Antidepressants can lift heaviness—but may not process grief.
- Anti-anxiety meds can soothe activation—but may not teach your system safety.
- Stimulants can boost focus—but may not address overload or nervous system imbalance.
- If you use medication, let it be **scaffolding** while you build the structure—nervous system regulation, emotional processing, trauma release, and lifestyle foundations. And **never** start/stop meds without your prescriber's guidance. Safety first, always.

AWARENESS WITHOUT RELEASE IS JUST RECYCLING PAIN.

#AWHOLEMOMENT

THE THERAPY TREADMILL (INSIGHT WITHOUT INTEGRATION)

Talk therapy can be powerful. Story matters. Meaning matters. But **insight without integration** is like reading about exercise and never moving your body.

You can understand your trauma and still get hijacked. That's not failure—it's physiology. The survival brain and body often **fire first**; the thinking brain comes online **after**. If the work never reaches the body, the loop continues.

Best-case therapy blends **story + skills + somatics**:

- Story: What happened matters.
- Skills: Regulation you can use when it counts.
- Somatics: Completing stress cycles in the body.

INSURANCE CONSTRAINTS (THE BOX WE'RE ALL ASKED TO FIT IN)

In many systems, to get coverage, you need a diagnosis. To keep coverage, notes must reflect ongoing symptoms. Sessions are time-boxed. Outcomes are often measured by symptom checklists, not **capacity** (connection, flexibility, resilience). Good clinicians do their best inside these constraints—but the box is real.

You're not wrong for needing care. Your therapist isn't wrong for documenting symptoms. The invitation here is simply: **don't confuse the paperwork with your potential.**

"WHY AM I STILL STUCK?" — A COMPOSITE STORY

Let's meet **Jessica** (name and details adjusted from many real journeys). Six years of care. Multiple diagnoses. Weekly therapy. Skills group. Med management. A full binder of effort.

"I'm doing everything right," she told me. "Why do I still feel broken?"

I asked a different question:

> "Has anyone ever told you that you can **heal**—not just manage?"

She cried. "No."

Jessica wasn't broken. The **approach** was. Once we began working with her **body's signals** (tight chest, shallow breath, clenched jaw), **completing stress cycles**, and **rewiring** the contexts that kept her system braced, the ground finally moved. She kept what helped (some therapy, short-term meds), added what was missing (nervous system training, grief work, boundary muscle), and her life expanded.

WHAT THE RESEARCH POINTS TOWARD (IN PLAIN ENGLISH)

I'm not here to argue headlines. I'm here to point you toward **principles** that consistently show up:

- **Expectation matters.** Belief, alliance with a trusted guide, and a felt sense of safety can drive a big slice of improvement. (Translation: relationship and ritual heal.)
- **Neuroplasticity is real.** Brains and bodies rewire with repetition, emotion, and environment. Patterns aren't permanent.
- **Somatic methods help.** Approaches that engage the **nervous system** (breathwork, EMDR, parts work with body awareness, bilateral stimulation, tremor release, cold/heat, vagal toning) often create faster, stickier change than insight alone.
- **Foundations matter more than we admit.** Sleep, movement, light exposure, nutrition, and community can dramatically shift mood and reactivity—because they alter physiology.
- Takeaway: **If the work reaches the body, the story can change.**

THE AWARENESS PARADOX

We've never had more mental health content. And yet distress rates keep climbing, especially for young people. Awareness is not the enemy; **awareness without embodied tools** is just a louder alarm.

We don't need less talk. We need **talk that leads to tools**—and practice that creates capacity.

THE NERVOUS SYSTEM ISN'T BROKEN. IT'S BRILLIANT AT SURVIVAL.

#AWHOLEMOMENT

A Humane Alternative (Without Throwing Anything Away)

This isn't "mental health vs. EQ." It's **mental health + EQ + body**. Keep what works. Add what's missing.

A complete approach looks like:

- Mind: language, meaning, beliefs, focus.
- Emotion: naming, allowing, moving through.
- Body: regulation, safety cues, and stress cycle completion.
- Context: boundaries, relationships, environment, purpose.
- Add **emotional intelligence** as the bridge: the skill of noticing what you feel, why it's here, what it needs—and responding with wisdom instead of reflex.

Case Windows (Short, Real, Relatable)

Rachel (elongated winter): Years on meds and in therapy. We treated her heaviness as a **shutdown response** to chronic overload. As she reclaimed sleep, light, and movement, processed grief in the body (not just mind), and rebuilt capacity, her prescriber supported a careful taper. "I wasn't broken. I was depleted and guarded."

Andre (rage spikes): Not "an angry person"—a nervous system stuck in **fight**. Learning to spot early cues (jaw, shoulders, breath), discharge activation safely, and repair after misfires changed his marriage more than a thousand apologies.

Maya (always "fine"): Lifelong fawning. Somatic boundary work + speaking micro-truths rebuilt a spine she thought she didn't have.

The Honest Audit (Your System, Your Story)

Part 1 — Inventory

- How long have you been "managing"?
- What labels do you hold? Which still feels helpful?
- Which tools actually change your day?
- What keeps you dependent?

Part 2 — Signals vs. Identity

- Write three phrases that shift identity to process:
- "I am anxious." → "I'm **experiencing** anxiety."
- "I am depressed." → "My system is **in shutdown** today."
- "I am broken." → "I'm **rebuilding capacity**."

Part 3 — Roots and Routes

- What current stressors keep your system braced (workload, screens, conflict avoidance, under-fueling, isolation)?
- What 2–3 *body-level* practices reliably help (breath cadence, walking outside, cold rinse, co-regulation hug, humming, bilateral tapping)?

Part 4 — The Boundary Promise

- One boundary you will keep this week for your nervous system health.
- "After 10 pm, no scrolling."
- "I will eat before coffee."
- "I will say 'I can answer that tomorrow' once this week."

Part 5 — Permission Statement

- Complete: *"I don't have to be a patient forever. I'm allowed to become ___."*

WHY YOU PICKED UP THIS BOOK (THE BIG SHIFT)

The old model whispers:

- "You are your label."
- "Coping is the ceiling."
- "This is just how you are."

The truth you'll practice here:

- **You are not your label.**
- **Coping is a bridge, not a home.**
- **Your system can learn safety, capacity, and joy.**
- You didn't do anything wrong. You're not behind. You just haven't had the whole map. Now you do.

Drop the Pack: "System Audit" Worksheet

1) Timeline of Care (1 page max):
Bullet your journey—what helped, what didn't, when you felt most like *you*.

2) What Your Body Says (today):
Circle where you feel stress **right now** (jaw, chest, gut, throat, shoulders). Put a star by the strongest signal.

3) Two Practices for 14 Days:
Choose exactly two **body-level** practices you'll do daily (5–10 min each). Track them. Non-negotiable.

4) The Conversation:
Tell one person you trust: *"I'm learning to heal at the root. If I look different—slower, quieter, firmer—it's on purpose."*

5) Review in Two Weeks:
Did your baseline change even a little? If yes—good. If no, simplify and try two different practices. Adjust the dials, not your worth.

Chapter 3 Key Takeaways

- The current model often **manages** symptoms; healing requires **root-level** work.
- **Labels can help**, but don't let them become identity.

- **Medication and therapy** can be essential supports; however, they're often **incomplete on their own**.
- Bringing **EQ and the nervous system** into the process turns coping into **capacity**.
- You don't have to choose sides. Keep what helps. **Add what heals**.
- You are not broken. You're **becoming**—and your body knows the way.

Chapter 3 Key Takeaways

- The current model of mental health often manages symptoms instead of healing the roots.
- Labels can clarify, but they can also cage.
- Medication and therapy can help—but by themselves, they're incomplete.
- Healing occurs when you incorporate emotional intelligence and nervous system work into the equation.
- You don't need to settle for management. You can heal

PART II:
THE SCIENCE OF
FEELING

Your Nervous System Is Running the Show

Here's the truth nobody told you in health class:
Most of your decisions, reactions, and "symptoms" aren't being run by your logical mind. Your nervous system is running them.

It's your **autopilot.**
Your **control tower.**
Your **smoke alarm and your security guard rolled into one.**

And once you understand how it works, you'll stop seeing yourself as broken—and start seeing yourself as brilliantly wired for survival.

THE SURVIVAL BRAIN VS. THE THINKING BRAIN

You've got two major operating systems inside you:

Survival Brain (Nervous System + Limbic System)

- Fast, automatic, body-first.
- Scans for danger 24/7.
- Fires before you can think.

Thinking Brain (Prefrontal Cortex)

- Slower, logical, conscious.
- Plans, reasons, solves problems.
- Comes online *after* survival has already reacted.
- This is why you can feel safe but still experience panic. Why can you promise you'll stay calm—and then snap. Why can you say, "I'm fine" while your body is screaming otherwise?

Your nervous system is running the show.

THE POLYVAGAL LADDER (THREE STATES YOU LIVE IN)

Dr. Stephen Porges' **Polyvagal Theory** provides a map of how the nervous system responds to safety or threat. Think of it like three rungs on a ladder:

1. **Ventral Vagal (Top of the Ladder)**
   - State: Safe, connected, social.
   - Body: Relaxed, open, steady breath.
   - Mind: Curious, creative, present.
   - This is where joy, love, and learning live.
2. **Sympathetic (Middle of the Ladder)**
   - State: Fight or flight.

- Body: Heart races, muscles tense, breath shallow.
- Mind: Narrow focus, survival thinking.
- This is where anxiety, anger, and urgency live.

3. **Dorsal Vagal (Bottom of the Ladder)**
   - State: Shutdown, freeze.
   - Body: Heavy, numb, low energy.
   - Mind: Hopeless, checked out, detached.
   - This is where depression and disconnection live.

Here's the kicker: you cycle these states all day long. It's not "good or bad"—it's biology. Problems happen when you get **stuck** in the middle or at the bottom.

Stress Cycles (Why You Can't Just "Get Over It")

Imagine a gazelle chased by a lion. Once it escapes, it shakes violently, takes a deep breath, and then returns to grazing. That's a completed **stress cycle.**

Humans? We rarely complete the cycle. We hold tension in our jaw, shoulders, and chest. We swallow grief. We override exhaustion with caffeine. We smile when we want to scream.

Result: trapped stress energy. Anxiety, depression, chronic pain, autoimmune issues—it all connects.

Trauma isn't just what happened to you. It's what got stuck in your body when it wasn't safe to finish the cycle.

YOU CAN'T THINK YOUR WAY OUT OF TRAUMA STORED IN THE BODY.

#AWHOLEMOMENT

PERSONAL WINDOW: AFGHANISTAN NIGHTS

When I got back from deployment, I told myself I was fine. I looked fine. My uniform was sharp, my salute was crisp, my smile was practiced.

But at night, my nervous system told a different story.
Shallow breath. Heart pounding. Sleep that never came.

It wasn't weakness. It was biology. My nervous system was still running the survival program it had needed overseas. My thinking brain couldn't talk it down.

The turning point came when I stopped asking, *"What's wrong with me?"* and started asking, *"What state am I in? What does my body need to feel safe again?"*

That shift changed everything.

EVERYDAY SIGNS YOUR NERVOUS SYSTEM IS RUNNING THE SHOW

- Snapping at your partner over nothing → Your survival brain says, "Fight."
- Freezing when you need to speak up → Your survival brain says "play dead."
- Overthinking every possible outcome → Your survival brain says, "scan for threat."
- Feeling nothing when you wish you could cry → Your survival brain says, "Shut down."

None of these means you're broken. They tell you your autopilot is active.

YOUR WINDOW OF TOLERANCE (HOW MUCH YOU CAN HANDLE BEFORE FLIPPING STATES)

Think of your nervous system like a window.

- Inside the window: regulated, resilient, present.
- Above the window: hyperarousal (anxiety, panic, anger).
- Below the window: hypoarousal (numb, disconnected, exhausted).
- The wider your window, the more you can handle without flipping into fight, flight, or freeze. The good news? Windows can expand.

SCIENCE MADE SIMPLE

- **Neuroception:** Your body constantly scans for safety or threat—without asking your permission.
- **Neuroplasticity:** Repetition and emotion can rewire your nervous system. Healing is possible at any age.
- **Co-regulation:** We regulate best with others. A hug, a calm voice, or a steady presence can reset your system.

You don't need to memorize the terms. Just know: your body is brilliant, your wiring is adaptable, and safety changes everything.

YOUR FREQUENCY IS WHAT YOU FREQUENTLY SEE

#AWHOLEMOMENT

SoulScience Alchemy in Action: Carla's Turning Point

Carla was a high-achieving executive who couldn't stop grinding. Her body was stuck in "on" mode—sympathetic overdrive. Chest tight. Poor sleep. Mood short.

Instead of talking her stress to death, we practiced something different: **pattern interrupts.**

- Two minutes of paced breathing.
- She shakes her arms and legs after meetings.
- A nightly "off switch" ritual (phone away, music on, body scan).
- Within weeks, she wasn't just "coping"—she was shifting states on purpose. Her team noticed. Her family noticed. Most importantly, she noticed.

Drop the Pack: Nervous System Check-In

Try this right now:

1. Pause. Breathe.
2. Scan your body: jaw, chest, gut, hands.
3. Name your state: safe, fight, flight, freeze.
4. Ask: *What would help me move one rung up the ladder?*
   - If anxious → exhale longer than you inhale.
   - If shut down → move your body, shake, step outside.
   - If braced → stretch, hum, or find a safe connection.

This isn't about fixing. It's about listening and giving your body what it needs.

Chapter 4 Key Takeaways

- Your nervous system runs survival programs before your brain catches up.
- You live on a ladder: safe, fight/flight, or shutdown.
- Trauma = incomplete stress cycles trapped in the body.
- You're not broken—you're brilliantly wired for survival.
- Healing involves widening your window of tolerance, allowing you to move with greater freedom.

CHAPTER 5

The Five Pain Languages That Shape Your Relationships

Y ou've probably heard of Gary Chapman's *Five Love Languages*—acts of service, words of affirmation, quality time, gifts, and touch. They blew up because they provided people with a simple, relatable way to talk about love.

But here's what nobody told us: when love breaks down, when we're hurting, we don't speak our Love Language, we speak our **Pain Language.**

Think of it this way: Love Languages are how we ask for connection. Pain Languages are how we cry out when connection feels threatened.

Pain Languages 101

Here's the big idea:

When we're hurting, our nervous system hijacks the conversation. We stop speaking from our higher self and start speaking from our wound.

And every wound has a dialect. I've seen five show up again and again:

1. **Anger** (*"Hear me!"*)
2. **Withdrawal** (*"I'm not safe."*)
3. **Control** (*"I can't trust."*)
4. **Perfectionism** (*"I'll never be enough."*)
5. **People-Pleasing** (*"Don't leave me."*)

1. Anger — The Fire Alarm

Anger gets a bad rap. But anger isn't the problem—anger is the smoke alarm. It's loud because something underneath feels unseen, unheard, or disrespected.

- What it looks like: yelling, sarcasm, "Why do I have to say this 10 times?"
- What it means: *"My needs matter too—please acknowledge me."*
- **Oh, That's Me:** Ever had someone slam a cabinet so hard you thought the kitchen owed them money? That's not about the cabinet. That's a Pain Language.

In Real Life: Anger is a surge of the sympathetic nervous system—adrenaline floods, the body braces, and fight mode activates. It's biology, not "bad personality."

2. WITHDRAWAL — THE TURTLE SHELL

Withdrawal looks calm from the outside, but inside, it's a survival shutdown. It says: *"Engaging feels unsafe. If I disappear, maybe I'll be okay."*

- What it looks like: silence, ghosting, "I'm fine" with dead eyes.
- What it means: *"I feel overwhelmed. I need safety before I can connect."*
- **Oh, That's Me:** If you've ever had a partner say "I just need space" and then take three days like they moved to witness protection—welcome to Withdrawal.

In Real Life: This is the dorsal vagal state (shutdown mode). The body numbs to conserve energy. Not laziness—biology.

3. CONTROL — THE AIR TRAFFIC CONTROLLER

Control looks bossy, but underneath it's pure fear: *"If I don't manage everything, it might all fall apart."*

- What it looks like: micromanaging, correcting, over-explaining.
- What it means: *"Chaos terrifies me. I need order to feel safe."*

- **Oh, That's Me:** You know the person who can't let anyone else load the dishwasher because "You're doing it wrong"? That's not just about plates—it's a Pain Language.

In Real Life: Control comes from hypervigilance. The nervous system is scanning for danger 24/7, trying to "fix" it before it happens.

4. Perfectionism — The Mask

Perfectionism looks polished but feels panicked: *"If I do it perfectly, maybe I'll finally be enough."*

- What it looks like: overworking, nitpicking, endless to-do lists.
- What it means: *"I'm terrified of failing and being unlovable."*
- **Oh, That's Me:** Ever proofread an email 17 times and still thought, "They're going to think I'm stupid"? Welcome to Perfectionism University. Tuition is a shame.

In Real Life: This is a survival-by-performance approach. The nervous system ties worth to output, keeping you in a state of constant sympathetic arousal (fight/flight).

5. People-Pleasing — The Smile That Hides

People-pleasing looks kind, but often it's fear in disguise: *"If I keep everyone happy, maybe I'll be safe."*

- What it looks like: over-accommodating, saying yes when you mean no, apologizing for existing.
- What it means: *"Rejection terrifies me. I'll sacrifice myself to stay connected."*
- **Oh, That's Me:** People-pleasers apologize to furniture. *"Oh, sorry, chair, didn't mean to bump you."* That's not politeness—it's programming.

In Real Life: Fawning is a trauma response. It's not weakness—it's survival through appeasement.

THE MIRROR PROBLEM

Here's why this matters: Pain Languages don't stay private. They trigger each other.

- Your **Anger** triggers their **Withdrawal.**
- Their **Control** triggers your **People-Pleasing.**
- Your **Perfectionism** triggers their **Anger.**

And just like that, you're not fighting about the dishes—you're fighting about childhood wounds reenacting themselves at 7:30 on a Tuesday night.

THE AWARENESS FLIP

When you know your Pain Language, you stop falling for the surface fight. You can say:

- *"This isn't about dishes. This is about me not feeling heard."*
- *"This isn't about bills. This is about me feeling unsafe."*

Pain Languages give you **translation power.** And translation is the first step to transformation.

MY PAIN LANGUAGE IN LOVE

For years, my Pain Language was Withdrawal. As a Marine, silence was armor. But in love, silence was gasoline. My partner wasn't fighting me—she was fighting the wall I built to survive.

The day I admitted to myself, *"I shut down when I feel unsafe,"* was the day the connection began. Not because I magically fixed it—but because we could finally name what was happening. Naming breaks the spell.

DROP THE PACK: DECODE YOUR PAIN LANGUAGE.

1. Think about your last three arguments. Write down your behavior.
2. Match them to the Pain Language list.
3. Ask: *What was the fear underneath?*
4. Now write what you actually needed.

Example:

1. Pain Language: Anger.
2. Underneath: I felt disrespected.
3. What I needed: To feel acknowledged.
4. Do this for you *and* your partner. Then compare. Warning: this may blow your mind.

PAIN IS A LANGUAGE. HEALING IS FLUENCY.

#AWHOLEMOMENT

Couples Challenge: The "Translation Game"

For one week, when conflict comes up, instead of saying:

- "You're so controlling!" → Say: "I hear you don't feel safe."
- "You never talk to me!" → Say: "I hear you feel overwhelmed."

You're not excusing the behavior—you're translating the language. And when people feel understood, they soften.

Why This Changes Everything

Love Languages tell you how to give love.
Pain Languages tell you how to heal love.

Both matter. But when things fall apart, the Pain Language is what's screaming in the room. If you can decode that, you hold the keys to connection.

Chapter 5 Key Takeaways

- Everyone speaks a Pain Language when they're hurting.
- The Five Pain Languages are: Anger, Withdrawal, Control, Perfectionism, and People-Pleasing.
- They're not flaws—they're survival strategies.
- They're contagious—your Pain Language triggers others'.
- Translation turns conflict into connection.

CHAPTER 6

Why Your Body Keeps the Score—But Your Soul Writes the Ending

I f you've been around healing circles, you've probably heard of Bessel van der Kolk's classic *The Body Keeps the Score.* It's one of the most quoted books in trauma research—and for good reason. It proved what many of us already felt in our bones: trauma doesn't just live in the mind, it imprints itself in the body.

But here's the part I need you to know:
Your body might keep the score, but **your soul writes the ending.**

That's the shift we're making in this chapter.

The Body Remembers, Even When You Forget

The body is like a black box on an airplane—it records everything. Even when your conscious mind tries to forget, your body remembers.

- Shoulders lock up when you hear your parents fight.
- Your chest tightens every time your boss sends "we need to talk."
- Stomach twists before dates because middle school rejection still echoes.

Velvet Hammer Truth: Your nervous system doesn't measure time in years. It measures time in patterns. If something *feels* like the past, your body responds as if it *is* the past.

The Scoreboard Isn't the Game

Here's where most people get stuck:
Because their body remembers, they assume they're doomed to relive it forever.

But let's make this clear: The scoreboard is not the game. It's feedback, not fate.

- Your nervous system says, *"This looks like danger."*
- Your soul says: *"But this is a new day. We get to choose differently."*

You are not locked in the replay. You are the author holding the pen.

SAY IT WITH YOUR CHEST.

When I came back from Afghanistan, my chest was a liar. Fireworks went off while I was driving on the 4th of July, and my body swore I was under attack. This was wild because it had never happened before. It's been 13 plus years since I retired, and this has never happened to me.

My brain knew I was safe. I was just driving on the freeway. But my chest didn't care—it screamed danger.

For months, I thought, *"This is just who I am now. Broken. Damaged. I'll never be normal again."* I was so embarrassed.

But eventually, I realized: my chest wasn't lying—it was protecting. It was saying, *"We've seen this before. We don't want you to die."*

That shift—thanking my body for trying to help—let me retrain it. I started saying, *"I hear you. But I'm safe now."* Over time, the fireworks stopped meaning war.

That's when my soul picked up the pen and rewrote the ending.

HOW THE BODY KEEPS SCORE (SCIENCE MADE SIMPLE)

Let's break down how trauma actually lives in the body:

1. **Amygdala Hijack:** Your amygdala (the smoke alarm) overreacts, firing before your thinking brain can weigh in.
2. **State-Dependent Memory:** You don't just recall facts—you recall *states*. If you're panicked, you remember other panics.

3. **Sensory Triggers:** Smells, sounds, sights instantly transport you to the original wound. (Ever smelled a cologne and been back in a toxic relationship in 0.2 seconds? Exactly.)

4. **Incomplete Stress Cycles:** Animals shake and discharge stress. Humans... file taxes, scroll Instagram, and shove it down. The cycle never completes.

PACK CHECK

- Ever snapped at your partner for chewing too loudly and realized halfway through it wasn't about the chips? Scoreboard.
- Ever laughed at pain to keep from crying? Scoreboard.
- Ever had your heart race when you received a "we need to talk" text? Scoreboard.

If you said, *"Oh, that's me,"* congratulations—your body's black box is online.

THE SOUL WRITES THE ENDING

The body may keep records, but your soul holds the pen. The soul says:

- "I am not my past."
- "I am not my pain."
- "I am more than my biology."

Your body remembers the betrayal.
Your soul learns boundaries.

Your body remembers the abuse.
Your soul learns resilience.

Your body remembers the breakup.
Your soul learns self-worth.

The soul doesn't erase the score. It reframes it.

TASHA'S RELEASE

Tasha had panic attacks in hospitals. As a child, she spent years visiting her sick parent. Her body kept vigil—every hospital smelled like grief.

She thought she was broken. But when we reframed it, she realized her body wasn't weak—it was loyal. It was saying, *"We suffered here before. I'll guard you now."*

Through somatic work, breath, and grief rituals, she kept the wisdom but dropped the weight. Hospitals became hospitals again, not haunted houses.

Her body kept the score, but her soul rewrote the script.

SCIENCE + SOUL IN PRACTICE

Here's how it plays out in real life:

- **Body:** Tight chest.
- **Soul:** "This is my body's way of protecting me."
- **Practice:** Breathe, thank your body, and remind it, *"I'm safe now."*

- **Body:** Stomach knots before public speaking.
- **Soul:** "My body remembers being humiliated in school."

- **Practice:** Shake it out, affirm: *"That was then. This is now."*

- **Body:** Jaw clenched during arguments.
- **Soul:** "This is my survival pattern."
- **Practice:** Soften the jaw, exhale, say: *"I can face this as my adult self."*

Your Nervous System Isn't an Enemy

Here's the reframe: your body isn't broken—it's brilliant. It just needs an update.

Think of it like an iPhone running on iOS 9. It's glitchy, slow, and keeps freezing. The hardware is fine—it just needs a system update.

Healing isn't deleting the old apps. It's upgrading the operating system.

Drop the Pack: Rewrite the Ending

1. **Identify** one body signal you feel often (tight chest, jaw clench, stomach knot).
2. **Ask it:** *"What are you trying to protect me from?"*
3. **Trace it:** What's the earliest memory you connect to that feeling?
4. **Rewrite it:** *"That happened. But I am safe now."*
5. **Rehearse it:** Each time the signal shows up, repeat the new ending.
6. Do this consistently, and your nervous system begins to believe your soul's script.

Your body remembers everything you try to forget.

#AWHOLEMOMENT

Bonus Practice: The Thank-You Ritual

Next time your body "overreacts," instead of fighting it, say:

- "Thank you for protecting me."
- "You don't have to carry this alone anymore."
- "I'm safe now."
- This flips the relationship. Your body stops being an enemy and becomes a partner in the healing process.

Chapter 6 Key Takeaways

- Trauma lives in the body through imprints, triggers, and incomplete stress cycles.
- Your nervous system measures safety by patterns, not calendars.
- The scoreboard shows the wounds, but doesn't dictate the outcome.
- Your soul reframes the story—turning wounds into wisdom.
- Healing = keeping the wisdom, dropping the weight, and writing a new ending.

PART III:
THE UNBURDENED
JOURNEY

CHAPTER 7

Recognize: Name It to Claim It

Y ou can't heal what you can't see.
You can't release what you can't name.

That's why the first step in transformation is always **recognition.**

WHY RECOGNITION MATTERS

Think about GPS. If you don't know your starting point, you can't get directions. Healing works the same way. If you can't name what you're carrying, you'll stay circling the same block, wondering why you never arrive.

The truth is: Avoidance doesn't erase pain—it just lets it run the show from backstage.

What We Don't Recognize, We Repeat

Have you ever noticed how the same type of person keeps showing up in your dating life? Or how the same fight keeps happening in your family, no matter the topic? That's not bad luck—that's unrecognized patterns playing out on repeat.

Pack Check 🐺**:** If your life feels like reruns, it's because the script hasn't been rewritten yet. Recognition is how you grab the pen.

The Science of Naming

Neuroscience refers to it as "affect labeling." Studies show that when you put words to emotions—literally saying, *"I feel anxious,"* or *"I feel ashamed"*—your amygdala calms down and your prefrontal cortex (thinking brain) comes online.

Naming the feeling doesn't make it disappear, but it takes it out of the driver's seat.

In Real Life: Next time you're spiraling, try whispering, *"This is anxiety."* Notice how your body shifts, even slightly. That's your nervous system saying, *"Thank you for naming me—I can stand down a bit now."*

The Backpack Got Loud

For years, I carried "anger" like it was my middle name. I didn't recognize it for what it was—grief. The child in me didn't have the language for sadness, so it came out as snapping, yelling, frustration, and sarcasm, or I would just shut down completely.

The day I named it— *"This isn't anger, this is grief"*—something cracked open. Recognition didn't erase the pain, but it gave me a way to cope. Instead of being hijacked, I could start to work with it.

That was the first brick in building freedom.

RECOGNITION ≠ OBSESSION

Let me be clear: recognition isn't about overanalyzing every move. It's not about living in therapy forever, circling the same stories until you drown.

Recognition is about honesty. It's saying:

- "I'm lonely."
- "I'm scared."
- "I'm carrying shame that isn't mine."

It's less about *why* you feel it and more about *owning* that you do. Once you see it, you can shift it.

HOW TO PRACTICE RECOGNITION

1. **Pause** — take 10 seconds before reacting.
2. **Scan** — check your jaw, chest, gut. Where's the tension?
3. **Name** — put words to it: anger, sadness, fear, shame, grief.
4. **Claim** — say, *"This is mine right now—but it doesn't define me."*
5. **Pack Check:** If you've ever said, *"I don't even know why I'm like this,"* recognition is the missing step.

COMFORT ZONES KEEP YOU SAFE. GROWTH ZONES SET YOU FREE.

#AWHOLEMOMENT

COMMON BLOCKS TO RECOGNITION

- **Busyness:** You can't recognize what you outrun.
- **Shame:** You avoid naming what you think makes you "bad."
- **Comparison:** You dismiss your pain because "others have it worse."
- **Denial:** You confuse not naming it with not having it.
- All of these keep the backpack zipped tight. Recognition is what unzips it.

TERRY'S BREAKTHROUGH

Terry was a leader who consistently motivated his team. He swore he had an "anger problem." But when we slowed down, he realized it wasn't anger at all—it was fear of being exposed as not good enough.

Once he named the fear, the anger started to dissolve. He could say, *"I'm scared I'll fail,"* instead of screaming about reports being late. Recognition shifted him from an attack mode to one of honesty—and his team followed.

DROP THE PACK: THE NAMING GAME

Try this right now:

1. Write down your top three recurring emotions this week. Example: frustration, sadness, exhaustion.
2. For each, write the trigger.
   - Frustration → "When people don't text back."
   - Sadness → "When I scroll social media."

     ○ Exhaustion → "When I pretend I'm fine."

3. Now write the translation:
     ○ Frustration → "I feel unimportant."
     ○ Sadness → "I feel like I'm behind."
     ○ Exhaustion → "I feel unsupported."

When you recognize the *real* emotion underneath, you stop shadowboxing.

The First "R" of R³

This is why Recognize comes first in the journey. It's not about judgment—it's about awareness.

When you name it, you claim it.
When you claim it, you can reframe it.
When you reframe it, you can release it.

Recognition is the doorway. Everything else flows from here.

Chapter 7 Key Takeaways

- You can't heal what you don't recognize.
- What you don't name, you repeat.
- Naming emotions calms the brain and creates choice.
- Recognition isn't about overanalyzing—it's about honesty.
- Once you name it, you can claim it—and from there, you can change it.

CHAPTER 8

Reframe: Turn Your Pain into Power

Recognition shows you what you're carrying.
Reframing changes how you carry it.

This is where we turn the same weight into a different story.

WHY REFRAME?

Two people can go through the same experience and walk away with two completely different lives. The difference isn't what happened—it's the meaning they made of it.

One person says, *"My parents' divorce ruined me."*
Another says, *"My parents' divorce taught me how to love differently."*
Same event. Different frame. Different freedom.

Real talk: Pain is inevitable. Suffering is often the story we attach to it.

DROP THE PACK. PICK UP YOUR POWER

#AWHOLEMOMENT

The Science of Reframing

- **Cognitive Reappraisal:** Psychologists have shown that when you reinterpret a stressful event, your brain activity actually shifts.
- **Neuroplasticity:** The more you practice a new perspective, the stronger that neural pathway becomes.
- **Memory Editing:** Every time you recall a memory, you have the chance to "update" it with new context.
- Reframing doesn't deny reality. It redefines it.

From Burden to Backpack

When I was younger, I thought my trauma made me weak—every outburst, every sleepless night, every failed relationship felt like proof that I was broken.

The reframe?
What if the weight wasn't punishment, but training?
What if every rock in my backpack was preparing me to help others put theirs down?

That one reframe shifted me from being a victim to being a vessel. My pain became my purpose.

Common Bad Frames We Live In

- **Frame 1: "I am broken."**

- o   Reframe: *"I am healing."*
- **Frame 2: "I failed."**
  - o   Reframe: *"I learned."*
- **Frame 3: "This always happens to me."**
  - o   Reframe: *"This is showing me what I still need to heal."*
- **Frame 4: "They ruined my life."**
  - o   Reframe: *"They revealed where I needed boundaries."*

Pack Check: If your story leaves you powerless, it's time for a reframe.

Okay, I know it's not just me.

- Ever bomb a presentation and think, *"I'll never recover"*? → That's a frame.
- Ever text someone and see the three dots disappear, then spiral? → Frame.
- Ever post something online and delete it after 2 minutes because no one liked it yet? → Frame.
- The story you attach is often heavier than the actual moment.

James Father Wound

James grew up with a dad who left when he was young. His frame was: *"If my father didn't stay, I must not be worth staying for."* That frame shaped every relationship.

When we worked together, I asked him: *"What if your dad's leaving wasn't about your worth, but about his wounds?"*

That single reframe cracked him open. He didn't excuse his dad—but he no longer carried the lie that he was unlovable. His relationships shifted. His identity shifted.

Recognition showed him the wound. Reframing gave him new eyes.

THE POWER OF LANGUAGE IN REFRAMING

Notice the difference between these statements:

- "I am depressed." → *Identity.*
- "I'm experiencing depression right now." → *Temporary state.*
- "I can't do this." → *Final.*
- "I haven't learned how to do this yet." → *Possible.*

Language is medicine. Sometimes, the most minor shift in words can completely rewrite the whole story.

THE FRAME FLIP EXERCISE

1. Write down one negative belief you keep repeating.
   - "I'm always messing things up."
2. Ask: What's the story underneath?
   - "If I fail, I'm worthless."
3. Flip it: Write a new frame that's true and freeing.
   - "Every mistake is data. I'm learning faster than most because I try."
4. Say it out loud daily until it feels natural.

The frame you feed is the frame that grows.

WHAT YOU'RE NOT HEALING, YOU'RE HELPING

#AWHOLEMOMENT

WHEN REFRAMING GOES WRONG

Not every reframe is healthy. Some people use "toxic positivity" to avoid real pain:

- "It could be worse."
- "Everything happens for a reason."
- "Just be grateful."

That's not reframing—that's repression with glitter.

In Real Life: True reframing doesn't skip grief. It honors it, then expands the story.

THE JOB LOSS SHIFT

Rachel lost her job and spiraled: *"I'm a failure."* We reframed it: *"This is a graduation, not a failure. The job ending isn't the end of your career—it's a redirect."*

Within months, she had secured a new role aligned with her passion: the same event, a new frame, and a different outcome.

ADVANCED REFRAMES (WHEN YOU'RE READY)

- **Reframe the Timeline:** "I wasted years" → "Those years taught me what I won't settle for."
- **Reframe the Relationship:** "They hurt me" → "They showed me my strength."

- **Reframe the Identity:** "I'm a mess" → "I'm in progress."
- **Reframe the Pain:** "This broke me" → "This broke me open."

DROP THE PACK: PAIN LANGUAGE REMIX

Remember Chapter 5? Imagine the Pain Languages without reframing:

- Anger: "I'm just an angry person."
- Withdrawal: "I'm cold and distant."
- Control: "I'm a control freak."
- Perfectionism: "I'm never good enough."
- People-Pleasing: "I'm weak."

Now reframe them:

- Anger → "I have passion that needs direction."
- Withdrawal → "I need safety before I can connect."
- Control → "I'm wired for leadership—I just need to trust more."
- Perfectionism → "I care deeply about excellence."
- People-Pleasing → "I'm gifted at empathy—I just need boundaries."

See how the same behavior shifts from shame to strength? That's reframing at work.

THREE FRAMES TO FLIP THIS WEEK

1. Choose one relationship, one memory, and one current challenge.

2. Write down your current frame.

3. Write a healthier reframe for each.

4. Share at least one with someone you trust.

CHAPTER 8 KEY TAKEAWAYS

- Reframing changes the meaning you attach to experiences.
- The brain literally rewires through repeated reframes.
- Bad frames make you powerless; new frames give you choice.
- Language matters: shift from identity labels to temporary states.
- True reframing doesn't bypass pain—it honors and expands it.
- The story you choose determines the life you live.

CHAPTER 9

Release: How to Finally Let Go

You've recognized the rocks. You've reframed their meaning. Now comes the part your soul has been craving — **release.**

Release is the moment you put the backpack down. It's when what you've carried no longer carries you.

WHY RELEASE MATTERS

Recognition without release is awareness without freedom.
Reframe without release is clarity without closure.

Release is the step that transforms healing from theory into reality.

Real Talk: You can't rise if you're still gripping the ground.

THE SCIENCE OF LETTING GO

Letting go isn't just a Hallmark phrase—it's biological.

- **Stress Cycle Completion:** When your body finally shakes, cries, trembles, exhales—that's your nervous system finishing the loop.
- **Memory Reconsolidation:** Research shows that when you revisit a memory with new meaning, the brain can literally overwrite the old emotional charge.
- **Forgiveness Studies:** People who practice forgiveness (whether spiritual or psychological) show lower blood pressure, reduced cortisol, and improved immune function.

Release is health. Release is freedom written into your biology.

THE BONFIRE

There was a night I sat at a bonfire with a rock in my hand. On it, I had written the word **"shame."** That rock felt heavier than anything the Marines ever made me carry.

When I threw it into the fire, nothing magical happened in the sky. But something shifted inside me. It was the moment I realized: I didn't need to keep carrying what was never mine to begin with.

That's release—not forgetting, not denying, but deciding the weight doesn't get to run your story anymore.

HEALING ALONE IS SURVIVAL. HEALING TOGETHER IS REVOLUTION.

#AWHOLEMOMENT

EVELYN'S LETTER

Evelyn had carried the betrayal of her ex-husband for 12 years. When she finally wrote him a letter—one she never sent—she cried for hours. The release wasn't in his reading. The release was in her *writing*.

When she burned it, she said, *"I thought the fire was destroying it. But really, it was transforming me."*

PACK CHECK

- Still replaying a conversation from 10 years ago in the shower? Backpack's still zipped.
- Still stalking your ex on socials just to prove you're "over them"? Pack check.
- Still blaming yourself for things you had no control over? Yup—that's weight.
- If your shoulders hurt more than your heart sometimes, it might not be posture—it's pain you haven't put down.

WHAT RELEASE IS NOT

- **It's not pretending it didn't matter.**
- **It's not forgetting.**
- **It's not excusing the harm.**

Release is choosing to stop letting the weight define your future.

RELEASE PRACTICES (TRY THESE)

1. **The Rock Ritual**
   - Write what you're carrying on a stone.
   - Hold it. Feel the weight.
   - Then throw it into water, fire, or dirt. Say out loud: *"This is not mine anymore."*

2. **The Letter You Don't Send**
   - Write everything you wish you could say to the person who hurt you.
   - Don't edit. Don't hold back.
   - Then burn, shred, or bury it. Release isn't about them—it's about you.

3. **The Breath Release**
   - Inhale: imagine drawing the pain up.
   - Exhale: release it through sound, sigh, or hum.
   - Repeat until your body softens.

4. **The Forgiveness Frame**
   - Not "It's okay."
   - Say: *"I release you so I can be free."*

WHEN RELEASE FEELS IMPOSSIBLE

Sometimes the weight feels as if it's fused to your bones. Here's what I need you to hear: that doesn't mean you're broken—it means you've been carrying too long.

Release doesn't always happen in one big dramatic moment. Sometimes it's daily micro-releases:

- Saying no.
- Crying for five minutes.
- Breathing deeper.
- Telling the truth to yourself.
- Release can be a waterfall—or a drip. Both erode the rock.

THE STUFF WE HOLD ON TO

We hold grudges like they're collectibles.

- That time your friend didn't text you back in 2012? Still in the vault.
- That middle school teacher who embarrassed you in front of the class? VIP section in your brain.
- That ex who blocked you, but you still peek at their Spotify playlists? Hall of Fame.

We laugh, but it's true. We hold onto things way longer than our nervous system was designed for. Release is about finally clearing storage space.

TYLER'S FREEDOM

Tyler grew up with an absent father. For years, he swore he'd never forgive him. That anger shaped his life.

When we worked together, I asked him: *"If you put this down—not for him, but for you—what would you finally be free to do?"*

He broke down. His answer? *"Be the father mine wasn't."*

That was the release. Not letting his dad off the hook and letting himself off the hook.

GUIDED RELEASE RITUAL

Tonight, before bed:

1. Write one burden on paper.
2. Hold it to your chest. Say: *"I see you. I carried you. But I don't need you anymore."*
3. Tear it into pieces.
4. Exhale. Sleep lighter.
5. Try this for seven nights. See what shifts.

DROP THE PACK: RELEASE IS NOT THE END— IT'S THE BEGINNING.

Release isn't about losing—it's about making space.

When you put the pack down, your hands are finally free to:

- Hold love.
- Build dreams.
- Catch blessings.

- Embrace joy without guilt.

Release is not the last chapter. It's the first chapter of who you're becoming.

CHAPTER 9 KEY TAKEAWAYS

- Release is the bridge from awareness to freedom.
- Letting go is a biological process: stress cycles, memory rewiring, and the science of forgiveness.
- Release isn't forgetting—it's choosing freedom.
- Rituals (rocks, letters, breath, forgiveness) help embody release.
- Release isn't always a single moment—it can be made up of micro, daily choices.
- When you release the weight, you make room for life to unfold.

PART IV:
HEALING OUT LOUD

CHAPTER 10

W.H.O.L.E.

Most people heal in silence. They cry in their car, journal in private, pray in secret, then show up in public with the mask back on.

I get it. The world taught us to suffer quietly. To "man up." To "keep it together." To "not air our dirty laundry."

But silence is heavy. Secrets are suffocating. And shame grows best in the dark.

That's why we need a new creed—a new way to live.

THE CREED: W.H.O.L.E.

W.H.O.L.E. = We Heal Out Loud Every day.

It's not just a slogan. It's a way of life.

- **We** → Healing isn't solo. It's collective.
- **Heal** → Not just manage, not just cope. Heal.
- **Out Loud** → Healing is witnessed. Healing is shared. Healing is contagious.
- **Every Day** → Not once a year on vacation. Every day. In micro-moments. In conversations. In choices.

This is the rhythm of a W.H.O.L.E. life.

Why Out Loud?

Because what we aren't healing, we're helping.
We're helping it by hiding it.

Silence says: *"I'm alone in this."*
Healing out loud says, *"Me too. We're in this together."*

Real Talk: You don't break generational cycles in isolation. You break them in community, in conversation, in courage.

The First Time I Said It Out Loud

For years, I was the strong one. The Marine. The motivator. The guy who could carry it all.

But the night I finally admitted out loud, *"I'm not okay,"* was the night my healing began. Saying it didn't make me weak—it made me free.

That's the power of out loud.

The Science of Out Loud Healing

- **Mirror Neurons:** When you share your truth, others' brains literally fire in sync. They feel with you. That creates a connection.
- **Co-regulation:** The nervous system calms more quickly in the presence of a safe companion than when alone. Out loud is medicine.

- **Shame Research:** Brené Brown found that shame thrives in silence but dissolves in empathy. Speaking truth breaks shame's grip.

Your body might carry pain, but your voice carries freedom.

PACK CHECK

Ever felt lighter after venting to a friend? That's out loud healing.

Ever joined a group and realized, *"I thought I was the only one"*? That's out loud healing.

Have you ever laughed through tears while telling your story? Out loud healing again.

You've already done it—you just didn't have a name for it.

HOW TO HEAL OUT LOUD (PRACTICAL STEPS)

1. **Name One Truth a Day**
   - Tell someone one honest thing daily. Doesn't have to be deep. "I'm tired." "I'm proud." "I need help."
2. **Find Safe Witnesses**
   - Choose people who can hold space, not judge. Out loud doesn't mean to everyone. It means to the *right* ones.
3. **Practice Micro-Bravery**
   - Share a story you'd usually hide. Speak a need you'd usually swallow.
4. **Celebrate Others' Out Loud**
   - When someone else shares, don't fix them. Just witness. Say, *"Thank you for telling me."*

HEALING IS CONTAGIOUS WHEN IT'S WITNESSED.

#AWHOLEMOMENT

The Movement of W.H.O.L.E.

This isn't just about you. This is about all of us. Imagine:

- Families where kids hear parents admit mistakes.
- Workplaces where leaders say, *"I'm struggling, too."*
- Communities where healing isn't hidden—it's modeled.
- That's the W.H.O.L.E. vision. Not perfection. Not pretending. Just humans healing out loud, every day.

Drop the pack: The Heal Out Loud Challenge.

This week, choose one moment to heal out loud:

- Tell a trusted friend about a fear you've never named.
- Share a win without downplaying it.
- Post a truth online that feels brave.

Notice the relief in your body when you speak. That's freedom echoing.

Chapter 10 Key Takeaways

- Healing in silence is heavy. Healing out loud is freeing.
- W.H.O.L.E. = We Heal Out Loud Every day.
- Out loud matters because connection regulates us and dissolves shame.
- One truth a day keeps the weight away.
- Healing is contagious—when you do it out loud, others find permission too.

HEALING OUT LOUD IS MEDICINE.

#AWHOLEMOMENT

CHAPTER 11

From Surviving to Thriving: The Growth Seekers Way

S urvival is important. Survival keeps you alive. However, survival was never meant to be the ultimate goal.

Too many people get stuck in a state of survival mode. They cope. They manage. They stay alive. But they don't feel alive.

Thriving isn't just breathing. Thriving is building. Thriving is becoming. Thriving is the way of the Growth Seekers.

SURVIVAL VS. THRIVING

Survival sounds like:

- "I just have to get through the week."
- "I can't let anyone see me fall apart."
- "If I stay quiet, maybe I'll be safe."

SURVIVAL KEEPS YOU ALIVE. GROWTH MAKES YOU ALIVE.

#AWHOLEMOMENT

Thriving sounds like:

- "What can I create this week?"
- "I can be real and still be loved."
- "I'm safe enough to grow."

Real Talk: Survival is about holding on. Thriving is about letting go and leaning forward.

THE SCIENCE OF THRIVING

- **Growth Mindset (Carol Dweck):** Thrivers see failure as feedback, not identity.
- **Post-Traumatic Growth:** Research shows trauma can catalyze greater meaning, strength, and relationships.
- **Neuroplasticity:** Your brain literally rewires through challenge and repetition. Thriving is training.
- You're not stuck with your old wiring. Your nervous system is designed for growth and expansion.

MARINE SURVIVAL, HUMAN THRIVING

The Marine Corps trained me to survive—scan for threats, stay alert, never let your guard down. That skill saved my life in combat. But in civilian life, survival became a cage.

It took me years to realize that thriving meant building trust, fostering connections, and cultivating a vision. It wasn't about scanning for threats—it was about scanning for opportunities. That reframe was the difference between living like a soldier and living like a seeker.

The Growth Seekers Creed

Growth Seekers don't settle for coping. We reach for more.

1. **Curiosity:** We ask questions others are scared to ask.
2. **Courage:** We take risks others avoid.
3. **Community:** We rise together, not alone.

Survival Mode Signs

- You know every Netflix intro song by heart.
- Your Amazon cart has more self-help books than your bookshelf.
- You say "I'm fine" with the same tone as "the Wi-Fi's down."

If that's you, you're surviving—not thriving.

How to Move From Surviving to Thriving

1. **Expand Your Window**
   - Survival shrinks capacity. Thriving widens it. Practice nervous system tools daily (breath, movement, co-regulation).
2. **Redefine Success**
   - Survival = avoiding pain and thriving = pursuing purpose. Write down what success *feels* like, not just looks like.
3. **Seek Growth, Not Comfort**
   - Comfort zones may feel safe, but they keep you stuck. Growth zones can feel scary, but they also expand your life.
4. **Build Your Tribe**

    ○   Thriving doesn't happen in isolation. Find Growth Seekers around you. Healing out loud is powerful—but *growing out loud* is transformation.

PACK CHECK

- If you say "just making it" every Monday, you're surviving.
- If you've had the same goals on your New Year's list for five years, you're surviving.
- If your body's alive but your soul feels numb—you guessed it—survival mode.

The good news? Thriving is available. Right now.

THE THRIVE LENS

Take one current struggle and ask:

- Survival question: *"How do I get through this?"*
- Thriving question: *"How can I grow from this?"*

Example:

- Survival: "My job is killing me."
- Thriving: "This job is showing me what I never want to settle for again."
- The shift in question reframes the whole story.

HEALING ISN'T THE CEILING. IT'S THE FLOOR.

#AWHOLEMOMENT

DROP THE PACK: THE THRIVING AUDIT

1. Write down three areas you're just surviving (work, love, health).
2. Circle the one that drains you most.
3. Write a survival statement: "I'm just getting by because..."
4. Flip it into a thrive statement: "I will grow by..."
5. Take one micro-action this week toward the Thrive version.

THE INVITATION TO GROWTH SEEKERS

Being a Growth Seeker isn't about being perfect. It's about being committed to learning, stretching, stumbling, and rising.

It's about asking more from life than "barely making it."

It's about daring to believe that healing is the floor, not the ceiling.

CHAPTER II KEY TAKEAWAYS

- Survival keeps you breathing. Thriving makes you alive.
- Thriving = curiosity, courage, community.
- Your brain and nervous system are wired for growth.
- Comfort zones keep you stuck; growth zones expand you.
- You don't have to settle for surviving—you were born to thrive.

CHAPTER 12

You Deserve It: Your Birthright to Wholeness

If nobody has ever told you this before, let me say it loud enough for your past, present, and future to hear:

You deserve it.
You deserve peace.
You deserve joy.
You deserve love that doesn't hurt.
You deserve freedom from shame.
You deserve mornings without dread and nights without regret.

Not because you earned it. Not because you proved it. Not because you finally checked all the boxes.

You deserve it because wholeness is your birthright.

WHOLENESS ISN'T A PRIZE. IT'S YOUR BIRTHRIGHT.

#AWHOLEMOMENT

THE LIE WE INHERITED

From childhood, most of us were handed a quiet script:

- *"Be smaller."*
- *"Be tougher."*
- *"Don't talk about it."*
- *"This is just who you are."*
- We were taught love is conditional. Safety is fragile. Belonging has strings attached.

Those scripts were lies. Your soul didn't write them. They were written by wounded parents, tired systems, unhealed ancestors, and cultures addicted to shame.

But here's the truth: you don't have to keep reading from that script. You get to write a new one.

THE BACKPACK IS DOWN

Consider where we began this book. You, carrying a backpack stuffed with Soul Weights—rocks labeled shame, anger, rejection, perfectionism, grief.

Page by page, we've unzipped it. You've recognized what's inside. You've reframed their meaning. You've released some of them into the fire.

Now, for the first time, you get to set the whole pack down.

Real Talk: The burden you thought was permanent was never yours to begin with.

Your hands are free now. Your back is lighter. Your soul can rise.

You don't have to carry what was never yours.

#AWHOLEMOMENT

FULL-CIRCLE TO MY 16-YEAR-OLD SELF

I dedicated this book to my 16-year-old self—the kid who thought toughness was survival, silence was safety, and pain was permanent.

If I could go back, I'd tell him:

- *"You're not broken—you're becoming."*
- *"This weight won't crush you—it will shape you."*
- *"One day, you'll help thousands unzip their packs too."*

I can't go back. But I can go forward. And so can you.

THE SCIENCE OF DESERVING

Worthiness isn't just spiritual—it's biological.

- Attachment Research: Infants are born expecting connection. You didn't come into the world thinking you had to *earn* love. You expected it because it's your design.
- Neuroplasticity: Your brain is built to rewire. No matter how many lies you learned, you can learn new truths.
- Positive Psychology: Studies show gratitude, purpose, and connection don't just make life "nice"—they extend it. Thriving is health.
- Forgiveness Research: People who release old hurts literally live longer, healthier lives.
- You were made to heal. You were wired to grow. Wholeness isn't a luxury—it's your factory setting.

WHAT WHOLENESS ACTUALLY LOOKS LIKE

Let's make it real. Wholeness isn't about never crying again, never feeling pain, or walking around glowing like a saint.

Wholeness looks like:

- Crying and not apologizing for it.
- Setting boundaries without guilt.
- Loving without losing yourself.
- Waking up curious instead of dreading the day.
- Feeling anger and channeling it into passion instead of destruction.
- Having bad days without believing you're a bad person.
- Wholeness is messy. Wholeness is human. Wholeness is free.

PACK CHECK (ONE LAST TIME)

Ask yourself:

- What am I still gripping that doesn't belong to me?
- Who gave me that rock?
- What would it feel like to set it down for good?
- Now, imagine your hands open. Imagine them free to hold love, to build dreams, to carry blessings instead of burdens.

That's what release makes possible. That's what wholeness feels like.

You don't need to be perfect to be whole.

#AWHOLEMOMENT

THE COLLECTIVE CALL

This isn't just about you. It's about us.

Because healing is contagious.
Because wholeness multiplies.

When you heal out loud, you permit your kids to heal out loud.
When you drop your pack, your family line gets lighter.
When you thrive, your community expands.

That's the W.H.O.L.E. movement. That's the Growth Seekers Way.
That's why this book is more than words—it's a revolution.

IMAGINE THIS

Imagine classrooms where kids learn Pain Languages alongside math.

Imagine workplaces where bosses say, *"I need help,"* and it's met with support, not shame.

Imagine prisons where men learn how to regulate their nervous systems instead of just serving time.

Imagine families where "I love you" and "I'm sorry" flow in equal measure.

That's what happens when we live like wholeness is our birthright.

DROP THE PACK: THE CLOSING RITUALS.

Here are three ways to seal this journey:

1. The Mirror Moment
   - Tonight, look in the mirror. Say out loud: *"I deserve it. I always have."* Keep saying it until your body believes it.
2. The Letter to Yourself
   - Write a letter to the younger you. Tell them: *"We made it. We're free. The pack is down."* Keep it as proof of your journey.
3. The Out Loud Affirmation
   - With someone safe, say the words: *"I'm whole."* Let them witness it. Healing out loud seals healing in.

THE FINAL REAL TALK

You've recognized.
You've reframed.
You've released.
You've stepped into W.H.O.L.E.
You've chosen growth over survival.

And now, you've remembered the truth you were born with: you deserve it.

Not tomorrow. Not once you prove yourself. Not when you finally "arrive."

Right now. As you are.

HELLO YOU

The pack is down. The shame is silent. The future is open.

And the rest of your story?

That's yours to write.

But let this book leave you with one sentence—tattoo it on your heart if you must:

You are not broken. You are becoming. You are W.H.O.L.E. You deserve it.

THE PHOENIX RISING

"You didn't survive all of that just to stay the same. You survived it to become unstoppable."

Y ou've reached the final pages of this book, but the truth is, your story is just beginning.

For too long, we've been told that the best we can do is manage our pain — cope with it, carry it, medicate it, talk about it. Those approaches can be helpful, but they don't provide the whole picture. What's been missing is **emotional intelligence** — the bridge that helps us move from surviving to thriving, from coping to healing, from silence to speaking out loud.

The good news? You don't need to wait for permission to rise. The power is already within you. Emotional intelligence is not a replacement for therapy or medicine — it's the missing piece that brings it all together. It's the puzzle piece that helps your mind, body, and heart finally work in harmony.

Healing doesn't mean forgetting the past. It means reframing it so it no longer defines you. It means releasing what was never yours to carry, and finally setting down the backpack of burdens you've had on your shoulders for too long.

Like the phoenix, you can rise from what once tried to burn you down. The ashes of old patterns, limiting beliefs, and inherited pain can become the soil of your rebirth. Every scar becomes proof that you survived — and an invitation to soar higher than before.

This is not the end, this is a call to action. To drop the pack. To recognize the weight. To reframe the story. To release what you no longer need. And most importantly, to **heal out loud** so others know they can too.

Remember:

- You are not broken. You are becoming.
- Healing isn't the ceiling. It's the floor.
- You don't have to be perfect to be whole.

THE TRUTH ABOUT TRANSFORMATION

Healing isn't a straight line. It's not a quick trip from broken to whole. It's more like a spiral — one that circles back to the same lessons, each time asking you to go a little deeper until the truth finally sticks.

You'll think you've released something, only to see it resurface in a new form. That doesn't mean you failed — it means you're ready to heal it at the next level.

You'll have breakthrough days followed by heavy ones. That doesn't mean healing isn't working — it means your nervous system is learning new rhythms, and sometimes it tests the old ones to make sure they're really gone.

You'll experience moments of profound freedom and then question yourself the next time pain shows up. That doesn't mean the transformation wasn't fundamental — it means healing requires space for both your healed self and your still-healing self to coexist.

The Phoenix doesn't rise just once. It rises again and again — every time you choose healing over hiding, growth over comfort, truth over protection.

WHAT I WANT YOU TO REMEMBER

If you take nothing else from this book, remember these truths:

You are not broken. You never were. You're a human being with a nervous system that's been doing its best to keep you safe in a world that hasn't always felt safe. Your anxiety, your depression, your trauma responses — they're not signs of weakness. They're intelligent signals from your body, reminding you of its desire to protect you.

What's often missing in the conversation is **emotional intelligence** — the piece that helps you move from coping to healing, from surviving to thriving. Emotional wellness is not a luxury. It's your birthright. The capacity for joy, peace, connection, and wholeness doesn't vanish because of stress or trauma. It simply gets buried under protective layers. Your work is to uncover it gently.

Healing occurs in both the body and the mind. You can't out-think trauma or over-analyze your way to wholeness. Your nervous system holds the key, and your body already knows the way forward. Learn its language. Trust its wisdom.

And remember — you're no longer carrying your burdens alone. Every rock in your backpack, every weight you've inherited or picked up along the way, can be set down. You can recognize what's yours, reframe how you see it, and release what no longer serves you.

Every time you choose healing over hiding, you're not only transforming your own life — you're shaping the lives of those around you. Healing is contagious. Your growth permits others to grow. Your wholeness becomes the spark that lights the way for someone else.

THE RIPPLE EFFECT OF YOUR HEALING

Healing doesn't just change you — it changes everyone connected to you.

Your partner no longer has to carry the weight of unprocessed anger. Your children don't inherit the same survival patterns you once lived through. Your clients, your team, your community — they don't get a wounded version of you. They get someone who has actually walked the road they're guiding others down.

When you heal, you break cycles. The trauma carried by generations before you doesn't keep flowing through you. You become the circuit breaker — the one who says, *"It ends here."*

When you heal, you permit others to do the same. People are watching — friends, family, co-workers, even strangers who simply notice your energy feels lighter. Your transformation whispers to them: *"If it's possible for them, it's possible for me too."*

When you heal, you contribute to the collective healing process. Wholeness is contagious. Every time one person steadies their breath, regulates their body, and chooses peace, the space around them shifts. Your healing doesn't just lift your load — it makes the world a softer, safer, and more whole place.

YOUR INVITATION TO RISE

This book isn't the end of your journey. It's the beginning.

Now that you know the truth — that you were never broken, that healing is possible, and that emotional intelligence is the missing piece — you have a choice to make.

You can close this book and return to old patterns that keep you stuck in a state of survival. You can stay in the comfortable discomfort of believing you need to be fixed.

Or you can rise.

You can commit to the practices in these pages. You can learn to regulate your nervous system. You can release inherited trauma. You can transform pain into wisdom and strength.

You can become your own healer.

This is your phoenix moment.

THE SoulScience Alchemy COMMITMENT

If you're ready to rise, here's the invitation:

Recognize your patterns. Notice when you're carrying someone else's baggage. Pay attention to which emotions are genuine responses to what's happening now, and which are echoes of inherited trauma. Keep asking yourself: *"Is this mine, or did I inherit this?"*

Reframe your relationship to difficult emotions. See anxiety as information. See depression as your nervous system conserving energy. View trauma responses as intelligent adaptations that once served to keep you safe. Let every feeling become a teacher, not a sentence.

Release what doesn't serve you. Make release a regular practice. Write down what you're ready to let go of — and create a ritual to mark it. Burn it, bury it, place it in water, or simply speak it out loud. The method matters less than the intention.

Regulate your nervous system daily. This isn't optional — it's foundational. Breathwork, movement, rest, meditation, nature, safe connection — find the practices that bring you back to center, and practice them consistently.

Heal out loud. Don't hide your journey. Share your struggles, your breakthroughs, your process. When you heal out loud, you remind others they don't have to carry their packs alone.

THE GROWTH SEEKERS MOVEMENT

You're not alone in this journey. There's a whole community of people choosing healing over hiding, growth over comfort, and authenticity over performance.

This is the Growth Seekers movement. We're people who believe wholeness is possible, who know we were created for more than survival. We're people who understand that our healing doesn't stop with us — it ripples into our families, our work, and our communities.

We Heal Out Loud Every Day.

That's not just a tagline. It's a commitment. It's a way of life.

It means showing up authentically, even when it feels uncomfortable. It means sharing your process, even when you're still in the middle of it. It means being honest about your struggles while celebrating your wins. It means choosing connection over perfection, progress over performance, becoming over pretending to have arrived.

This is what it means to be a Growth Seeker — not to have all the answers, but to be willing to live the questions out loud.

THE LEGACY YOU'RE CREATING

Here's something worth sitting with: you're building a legacy right now. Not someday. Not when you "arrive" or when you're finally "done healing." Right now. With every choice you make. Every time you pause instead of reacting. Every time you drop a weight that was never yours.

That's legacy.

So ask yourself:
Are you passing forward the pain you inherited, or are you breaking the chain?
Are you teaching your children that emotions are something to fear, or are you showing them that feelings are safe to feel and powerful to navigate?
Are you carrying forward the belief that healing is out of reach, or are you proving — through your very life — that transformation is always possible?

Because legacy isn't built in the future, it's written in the small moments of today.

And just like the Phoenix, you don't rise only for yourself. You rise to light the way.

MY PROMISE TO YOU

I promise to keep showing up. To keep teaching SoulScience Alchemy™. To keep putting the backpack down with you, one rock at a time. To keep sharing the tools, practices, and stories that remind you of what's possible.

Not because I've mastered it all — but because I know the weight of believing you're broken. I see the exhaustion of carrying pain that was never yours. I know what it feels like to think survival is all you'll ever have.

And I also know what it feels like to rise.

I've lived it. A kid from California who grew up surrounded by violence. A Marine who went to war — and came back with a nervous system locked in survival mode. A man who thought pain was permanent... until he discovered it didn't have to be.

If healing was possible for me, it's possible for you.

Your story won't look like mine. Your wounds, your journey, and your timing will be different. But your birthright is the same. Wholeness is already yours. And I promise to keep reminding you of that until you believe it for yourself.

THE BACKPACK OF BURDENS RELEASE

Before we close this journey together, I want you to try something with me.

Close your eyes. Imagine the backpack you've been carrying all this time — the one heavy with pain, shame, and survival. Feel its weight pressing down on your shoulders. Notice how tired you are from carrying it.

Now, slowly reach back and unzip it. One by one, take out the rocks you've been holding: the anxiety rock. The depression rock. The shame rock. The trauma rock. The inherited pattern rocks. Name them as you set them down. With every rock you release, feel the relief in your body.

When the backpack is empty, take it off completely. Lay it at your feet. Stand tall. Roll your shoulders back. Inhale deeply, like your lungs have more room than they've ever had before.

Notice the lightness. Notice the freedom. Notice that this ease isn't something new — it's who you've been all along, beneath the weight.

This is your natural state. This is the healed you that's been waiting underneath it all.

Now open your eyes. Remember: that feeling of lightness isn't imaginary. It's available to you, moment by moment, every time you choose to set the pack down.

YOUR WINGS ARE READY

The phoenix doesn't rise because the fire is easy. It rises because it knows transformation requires letting go of what no longer serves, so the truth of who you are can emerge.

You've walked through the fire. You've faced your patterns, your pain, your survival stories. You've unzipped the backpack and set the rocks down.

Now it's time to rise.

Your wings are ready. Your strength is proven. Your wisdom is earned.

You don't need permission. You don't need validation from systems or approval from people still carrying their own weight. You just need to choose to rise — and keep choosing it, every single day.

And when you rise, you don't rise alone. You rise for your children, your partner, your community. You rise for the people watching who need proof it's possible. Because that's what the Phoenix does — it doesn't rise just for itself. It rises to light the way.

Welcome home to yourself. Welcome home to wholeness.

THE JOURNEY FORWARD

If you've dropped some weight, keep practicing.
If you've uncovered your Pain Language, keep translating.
If you've remembered your birthright to wholeness, keep walking in it.

You weren't made just to survive, you were made to thrive.

THE FINAL WORD

You are not broken. You are becoming.

The pack is down. Your hands are free.
And your future is wide open.

Step forward lighter.
Step forward stronger.
Step forward whole.

This isn't the end.
This is the beginning.

You've always been W.H.O.L.E.

Now you know it

Acknowledgments

No book is written alone, and this one especially wasn't. These pages may carry my name on the cover, but they carry the fingerprints of every person who poured into me, believed in me, or challenged me along the way.

First, to my partner, Melissa — my Freckles. You've seen me at my highest and my lowest, and you've loved me through both. Thank you for reminding me daily that love is healing, and that partnership can be the soft place we land and the launchpad from which we rise. This book is as much yours as it is mine.

To my children — you are my legacy and my why. Every word I write, every rock I drop, every pack I set down — it's for you, so you don't have to carry what I did. May your lives be lighter because I chose to heal out loud.

To my 16-year-old self — we did it. The boy who thought he had to carry it all alone is now the man who teaches the world to put it down. Thank you for surviving long enough to let me thrive.

To my big brother — the one who stepped in and stepped up. Two years older, but somehow always miles ahead. You gave me someone honest to follow when all I had were TV dads, comic books, and Anime. You weren't perfect, but you were present. You made survival feel cool, and laughter feel like medicine. Our language has always been jokes and movie quotes, but the truth underneath has never needed translation. Ditto... Always.

To my mentors, coaches, and teachers — the ones who believed in me before I believed in myself — you know who you are. Your wisdom, your challenges, and your "velvet hammers" shaped me more than you know.

To my brothers and sisters in arms and to my fellow Marines — thank you for teaching me resilience, discipline, and loyalty. And to those we lost along the way: I carry you with me in every word, every speech, every moment of purpose.

To the Growth Seekers, clients, and community who trusted me with your pain — thank you. Every story you've shared has sharpened this message, humbled me, and reminded me why this work is so important. You gave me the honor of witnessing your healing, and in doing so, you also healed me.

And finally, to the reader — you. Thank you for letting me into your story, your pain, your hope. Thank you for turning these pages with courage, for healing out loud with me. I don't take your trust lightly. This isn't just a book — it's a movement we're building together.

From the bottom of my heart: thank you.

Stay W.H.O.L.E. Stay rising. And always remember — **you deserve it.**

— Maximus Lerois

Next Steps on Your Journey

You've set the pack down. Now it's time to keep walking lighter, stronger, and W.H.O.L.E.

Join the Growth Seekers Academy

Scan the QR code to connect with Maximus and a community of people healing out loud together: weekly coaching, tools, and conversations — all designed to help you rise.

EXPERIENCE WELLTHY RETREATS

Let go of what no longer serves you and rise renewed. Whether it's in the desert, by the ocean, or among the trees, Wellthy Retreats are designed to help you burn down old patterns and reset your nervous system at a soul level.

Scan the QR code to apply and be the first to know when the next transformational experience is announced.

STAY PLUGGED IN

Want weekly encouragement and tools to keep growing? Scan the QR code to subscribe to Maximus's YouTube, podcast, and newsletter.

Healing doesn't end with the last page. This is your beginning.

About the Author

M aximus Lerois is a Chief Wellness & Performance Strategist, Psychotherapist, and U.S. Marine veteran. A certified practitioner in Emotional Intelligence and Neuro-Linguistic Programming, Maximus has helped thousands Recognize, Reframe, and Release the emotional weights holding them back.

Through his SoulScience: Alchemy™ framework, Growth Seekers Academy, Wellthy Retreats, and global speaking engagements, he empowers people to heal openly and rise into their highest, most healed selves.

Blending real-world grit with neuroscience-backed tools, Maximus's mission is simple: to prove that you were never broken — and to remind you that wholeness is your birthright.